For Noa Krikler and the children who helped make this book:
Tommy Graham, Georgie Abbott, Alice Softly, Alfie Beecher,
Ella Krikler, Abel Rubinstein, Shannon Noone, Mia Aylott,
Joshua Shaffer, and Jake Couch

Copyright © 2001 Zero to Ten Limited
Photographs copyright © 2001 Sally Smallwood
Text copyright © 2001 Sally Smallwood

Publisher: Anna McQuinn
Art Director: Tim Foster
Senior Editor: Simona Sideri
Publishing Assistant: Vikram Parashar

First published in Great Britain in 2001 by Zero To Ten Limited
327 High Street, Slough, Berks SL1 1TX

A CIP catalogue record for this book is available from the British Library.

ISBN 1-84089 193-9

Printed in Hong Kong

CAN YOU SEE IT?
RECTANGLE!

SALLY SMALLWOOD

RECTANGLES

ARE
BRILLIANT!

A bit like a square – they have four sides and four corners – but two sides are long and two sides are short. Turn the pages and see how many you can find!

Here's one to wave

...and here's one
to wash with!

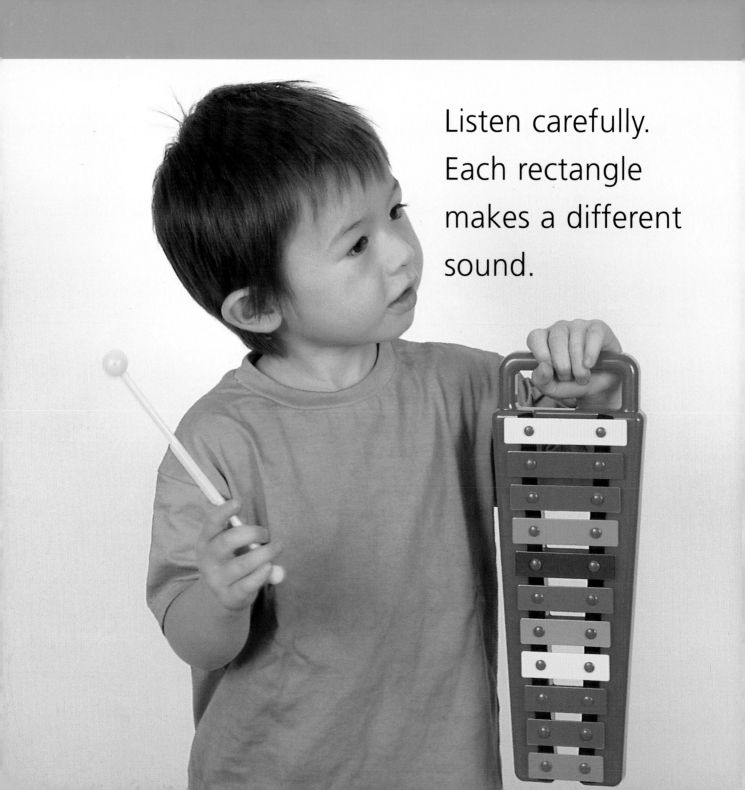

Listen carefully.
Each rectangle
makes a different
sound.

My rectangle's
yummy!

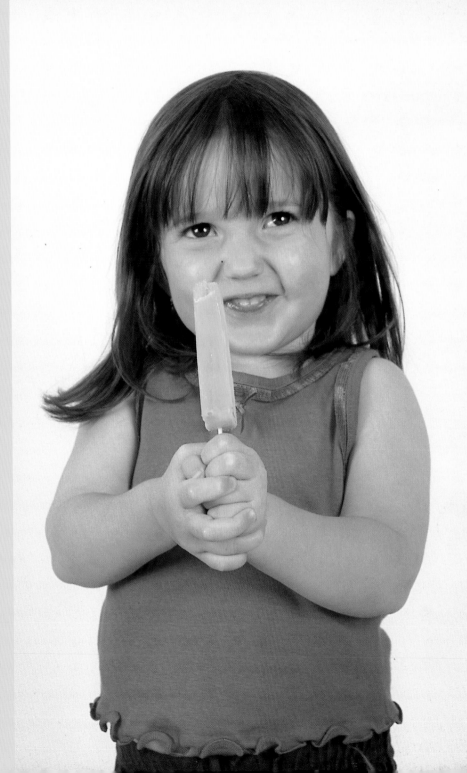

Clothes on the line –
rectangles all over
the place!

I think there's something in here for me...

Surprises often come in rectangles!

Here are lots and
lots of them...

I draw on my
rectangles.
Do you?

Sometimes you can find money...

in rectangles!

Rectangles are everywhere.
Can you find them?
Can you make some of
your own?